I0164801

BUKOWSKI

ERASURE POETRY ANTHOLOGY

BUKOWSKI

ERASURE POETRY ANTHOLOGY

Edited by

Melanie Villines

SILVER BIRCH PRESS
LOS ANGELES, CALIFORNIA

© COPYRIGHT 2014, Silver Birch Press, ALL RIGHTS RESERVED

ISBN-13: 978-0692278109

ISBN-10: 0692278109

FIRST EDITION: October 2014

Email: silver@silverbirchpress.com

Web: silverbirchpress.com

Blog: silverbirchpress.wordpress.com

Cover art by Loren Kantor (woodcuttingfool.blogspot.com)

Mailing Address:
Silver Birch Press
P.O. Box 29458
Los Angeles, CA 90029

Note: Authors retain all rights to their poems. If you wish to contact one of the poets, send an email to silver@silverbirchpress.com and we will forward the message.

INTRODUCTION

Melanie Villines

In 2013 and 2014, Silver Birch Press issued several calls for submissions for erasure poetry—poems created with words and phrases from books, magazines, newspapers, and other printed sources. We requested erasure poems based on various themes—fashioned from pages in hardboiled detective fiction (*NOIR Erasure Poetry Anthology*, December 2014), page 214 (Valentine's Day Poetry Series) and page 41 (April Fool's Day Poetry Series) of any book, and a Celebrity Free Verse Poetry Series with poems composed of words and phrases from celebrity interviews.

The previously mentioned erasure poetry projects were mostly a lark—enjoyable and entertaining. But the thought of creating erasure poems from a writing icon such as Charles Bukowski gave us pause. Would the resulting poems represent an homage? Or should we never consider messing around with Bukowski's revered works?

We decided to err on the side of trying, and seeing what came from this endeavor—and the result is the Silver Birch Press *Bukowski Erasure Poetry Anthology*.

The forty-one poets who contributed to this collection used Bukowski's novels, poetry, and letters as source material. All of the poets have high regard for Bukowski's work and approached this exercise with respect and even awe.

So, with love and appreciation, we dedicate this collection to Charles Bukowski, who has inspired so many writers to keep writing and so many people to keep living.

CONTENTS

things are so easily lost.
things just can't be kept forever.

CHARLES BUKOWSKI, White Dog

BUKOWSKI

ERASURE POETRY ANTHOLOGY

useless things

shake him

w

h

a   t

If the whole world

swallowed

three cans of beer

SUZANNA ANDERSON

useless things
    shake him

w

    h
        a   t

If the whole world

    swallowed

three cans of beer

SOURCE: "Hideaway" (poem), page 220, *Betting on the Muse: Poems & Stories* (Black Sparrow Press, 1996).

bluebird

wants

you.

out

but

know

s

you want to

asleep.

then I

sing a little

secret

do

you?

14

TARA R. ANDREWS

bluebird tweets

bluebird
wants
to let
you
out
but
knows
you want to
sleep
then I
sing a little secret
do
you?

SOURCE: "the bluebird" (poem), page 120, *The Last Night of the Earth Poems* (Ecco, 2002).

                You

        Won't

                              die   of

            divorce   She   told me

                    she   stretched
out on   my eyes
            pulling   one
then the other.   to   dress   up
shut off the   light

                            love   had a
                    chest   , it had doors,

                tiny   soft
things
        and   pieces of paper.   I
took the pieces of paper and looked at them.

BETH AYER

That Purple Something

You won't die
of divorce
she told me

She stretched out
on my eyes
pulling one
then the other.

to dress up
shut off the light

Love had a chest,
it had doors,
tiny soft things
and pieces of paper.

I took the pieces of paper
and looked at them.

SOURCE: *Women* (novel), page 12 (Ecco, 2007).

JENNI B. BAKER

a pretty woman

a
pretty woman
a little sun
another day
a gallon of gas
a
fear and madness
drying out
another
American writer

SOURCE: *Dangling in the Tournefortia,* page 8 (Black Sparrow Press, 1981).

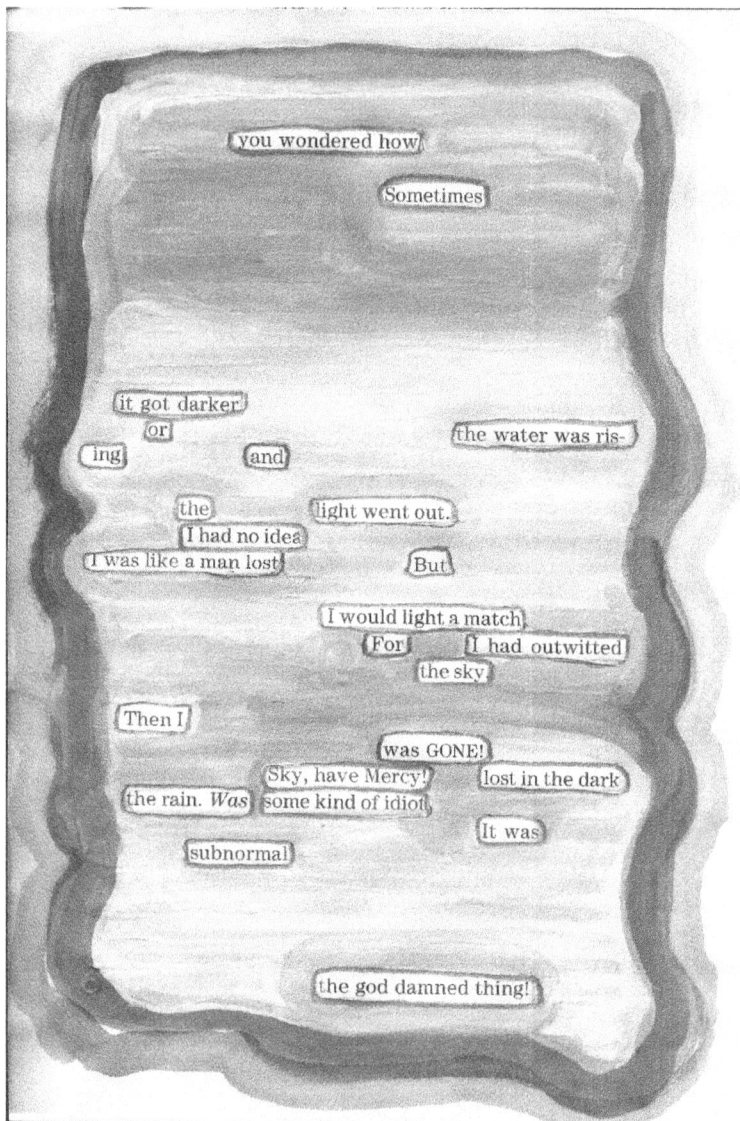

you wondered how

Sometimes

it got darker
or   the water was ris-
ing   and

the   light went out.
I had no idea
I was like a man lost   But

I would light a match
For   I had outwitted
the sky

Then I

was GONE!
Sky, have Mercy!   lost in the dark
the rain. *Was* some kind of idiot,
subnormal   It was

the god damned thing!

DAVID BARKER

lost in the dark

you wondered how
sometimes
it got darker or
the water was rising and
the light went out.
I had no idea. I was like
a man lost but
I would light a match
for I had outwitted the sky.
then I was GONE!
sky have Mercy!
lost in the dark.
the rain was
some kind of idiot.
it was subnormal,
the god damned thing!

SOURCE: *Post Office* (novel), page 27 (Black Sparrow Press, 1971).

. for   months, baby
          an old guy like me

                  talk about biting iron

                          yeah

          aching to   roll   on the floor

                  for anything

                                  with

  raison d'être
     a parlay

              like bottled sunlight   the breath of life

                      to think   about the
      present   sympathize with all
         who

                              long

MARY BAST

for months, baby

      an old guy like me

    talk about biting iron

   yeah

aching to

         roll

           on the floor

   for anything
        with
raison d'etre

   a parlay

  like bottled sunlight

         the breath of life

     to think   about the
present
           sympathize with all
  who

    long

SOURCE: "A Gigantic Thirst" (poem) pages 290-291, *The People Look Like Flowers at Last: New Poems* (Ecco, 2007).

The perfect poem will ▮▮▮ be
written▮

▮▮▮▮▮▮▮▮▮ at
11:00 a.m.,
▮▮▮▮▮
▮▮ to ▮▮▮
▮▮▮▮▮▮▮▮
the world.

The perfect poem will ▮▮▮ be
written▮
▮▮▮▮▮▮

here
▮▮▮▮▮▮▮

in the street,
on the wall.
▮▮
▮▮
▮▮▮▮
▮▮▮▮
▮▮▮▮
▮▮▮▮▮

The perfect poem will ▮▮▮ be
written▮

for this let us thank
the gods.

ALESSANDRA BAVA

The Perfect Poem Will Be Written

the perfect poem will be
written
at 11 a.m.
to the world

the perfect poem will be
written
here,
in the street,
on the wall.

The perfect poem will be
written
for this,
let us thank the gods.

SOURCE: "The Dangling Carrot" (poem), page 247, *Bone Palace Ballet* (Ecco, 2002).

the streets of
death,
death
can frame
your feet
make a broken mind
fly,
shake hands
with the devil
and win
almost anything,

BRINDA BULJORE

the streets of death

death
can frame
your feet
make a broken mind
fly,
shake hands
with the devil
and win
almost anything.

SOURCE: "Defining the Magic" (poem), page 131, *Betting on the Muse: Poems & Stories* (Ecco, 2002).

try

the waste
continues

as the waiter runs by

      the   white boys   laugh at
us.
no matter. no matter,
      your shoes are tied and
nobody is walking
behind.
just being able to
be nonchalant is victory

     constipated minds   seek
larger meaning

garbage

  will find
you.

KATHY BURKETT

Try

the waste
continues
as the waiter runs by.
the white boys laugh at
us.

no matter, no matter,
your shoes are tied and
nobody is walking
behind.
just being able to
be nonchalant is victory.

constipated minds seek
larger meaning.

garbage
will find
you.

SOURCE: "The Harder You Try" (poem), page 70, *The People Look Like Flowers at Last* (Ecco, 2007).

self-doubt, self-doubt
I often   write

                    think

and live   my own way.

    I   do not

               believe much

                                    click

of   keys   torn shade
    my face   clean white thunder.   I
like

        classical

                singing

            purified
        like the human voice

                        like the violin

played by human

                            fingers

TOBI COGSWELL

Doubt, Self-Doubt

I often write, think, and live my own way. I do not believe
much—
click of keys, torn shade, my face, clean white thunder.
I like classical singing, purified like the human voice, like the
violin, played by human fingers.

SOURCE: *Screams from the Balcony, Selected Letters 1960-1970*, Edited by
Seamus Cooney, page 65 (HarperCollins, 2003).

I had a hit   and I felt a
little better.   I
wasn't dead yet,

                    The man who
never carried extra luggage.

                         Go backwards and Nirvana

    I had another hit

Then the phone

        all the shit

                lousy philosopher   Death.

                        delusions

Hell

            it all worked out.

                    meet me at Musso's tomorrow

SUBHANKAR DAS

Meet Me at Musso's

I had a hit
and I felt a little
better
I wasn't dead yet
The man who
never carried
extra luggage
Go back-
wards and Nirvana
I had another hit
Then the phone
all the shit
a lousy philosopher Death
delusions
Hell
it all worked out
meet me at Musso's tomorrow

SOURCE: *Pulp* (novel), page 87, (Ecco, 2002).

██████ **Oranges**

first time my father ████████████████████
     bit of music ████████████████

it's called Love ████████████████

     I preferred ████

the most horrible thing

     part of me being
      ejaculated out of ██

stupid
I will ████ forgive him

     kill the Father

I.

MELISSA ELEFTHERION

Oranges

first time/my father
bit of music
it's called Love

i preferred
the most horrible thing
    part of me being
    ejaculated out of
stupid
I will/forgive him

Kill the father,
I.

SOURCE: "Three Oranges" (poem), *On the Bus* (1992).

A GREAT WHITE LIGHT

TRADITIONS PRESERVED
SOMETIMES
THE ANSWERS
ARE OUT OF MIND

THE LEADERS OF THE PAST
CURL UP TIGHTLY AT NIGHT
WAITING FOR THEIR GRACE

THE SAME OLD ACTORS
WATCH OUR FATHERS
WATCH OUR MOTHERS
PREPARED TO IGNORE
OUR SPIRITS

EXCEPTIONS
TEETER ON THE
EDGE OF ANY MOMENT
THE REST
OF US
RAVING AND BATTERED

SOMETHING IS KNOCKING
IT DAWNS ACROSS THE
CONTINENT

THE FLOWERS OPEN IN THE WIND
THE 21ST CENTURY
OUT OF REACH

36

MARK ERICKSON

a great white light

traditions preserved
sometimes
the answers
are out of mind

the leaders of the past
curl up tightly at night
waiting for their grace

the same old actors
watch our fathers
watch our mothers
prepared to ignore
our spirits

exceptions
teeter on the
edge of any moment
the rest
of us
raving and battered

something is knocking
it dawns across the
continent

the flowers open in the wind
the 21st century
out of reach

SOURCE: "Something's Knocking at the Door" (poem), page 212, *Slouching Toward Nirvana* (Ecco, 2006).

I see
your hands   tiny
and   in France
where you wrote

poems about

famous
lovers
jealous
because we'   never   got close

what you found out
is
fame —

is dead,
maybe.
you were   the
best
I loved you
like a man loves a woman he never touches, only
writes to, keeps little photographs of.

you said

you sat   crying
every night
hurt and forgotten   . I wrote
of your suicide

like this.

ALEXIS RHONE FANCHER

Love Letters from Paris

I see your hands,
small, and in France
where you wrote poems
about famous lovers –
most of them jealous
because we got close.

What you found out is
fame is dead.
Maybe.

You were the best. I loved
you like a man loves a
woman he never touches,
only writes to, keeps
little photographs of.

You said you sat crying
every night, hurt and
forgotten.

I wrote of your suicide like this.

SOURCE: "An Almost Made Up Poem" (poem), *Love Is a Dog from Hell*
(Ecco, 2002).

It was 2:15 p.m. I was holding down ██████████████████ ███ a vodka-7 ████████████████████████████ ███████████████████████ Business was good ███ just without direction. Guy ████████████████████ kept staring at me. ██████ people stared, ████████, like cows. They didn't know ███████████████ I ████ hit ◼ my vodka, ███████████ looked up. Guy ███ still staring. ████████ ██ ███████████████

███ stood up ████ started walking ██████████████. I checked my holster. ████████████. Snug. ████ best hard-on ██ man could have. Guy looked like ████████████████ ██████████████ a dentist. ███████████ ugly mustache ████ ◼ false smile. ████████████████████████████████ ████████. He got close ██████████ stopped, loomed ████

"Look, buddy," I said, ███████████ I don't have any loose change."

"I'm not hittin' you for coin, baby," ████████████ ██████████████████████ eyes like a dead fish.

JEFFREY GRAESSEY

Snug

it was 2:15 p.m.
I was holding down
a vodka-7,
     business
     was   good
just without

direction.

guy kept staring at me
people stared,
     like cows
they didn't know.

I hit my vodka,
looked up. guy
still staring
stood up, started walking

I checked my holster, snug
best hard-on man could have.

guy looked like a dentist
ugly mustache false smile

he got close, stopped,
     loomed

"look, buddy," I said,
"I don't have any loose change."

"I'm not hittin' you
for coin, baby."
     eyes
like dead fish

SOURCE: *Pulp* (novel), page 106 (Ecco, 2002).

the condition

▲▲▲

xkkxapxanxkxdxwxxxtbxexxxxxexxxxesx
xkxxxpexxphexaxxexixx pain
xtheyxsbexpxix pain xtbxeyxawxxkexxx
ixx pain
exvexxxhxxbxxkxxkxxgxxxxexxxx pain
xkxxxbxxdxgxsx
xkxxxfkxxwexxxxxxxxix pain
xxxxkxkxxxxxxixxxxxxxkexxxxxx
xxxxxx sits
xxxxxx floats
xxxxxx waits
xxxxxx is

don't ask why xkxxxxxxxxxx
xkxxxxkxs
xkxxxgxxxkkdixxtx
xxkxxkxxx

xkxxxxxxxsxxxixxkxxdx
xxxkxxkxx love
xxxkxtkxxxxsxxxipxtx

xkxixsxxkxxxxexxxxxxx
xxxkxtxxpxexxkxixxx

xxxxxxxx xyxxxxxxxxkxtkxixxx
xyxxxxxx pkxxxxx now

S.A. GRIFFIN

the condition

pain
pain
pain

pain

pain

sits
floats
waits
is

don't ask why

love

now

SOURCE: " the condition" (poem) *War All The Time: Poems 1981-1984*, page 150, (Black Sparrow Press, 1984).

private
flame
poor
conceited,   comedians.

Known

by   gray man
who   fondles
the night
longer   e
than all
bomb   throats
in a

smoke   cloud
cat walk   shakes
like wax: spines
and our consciousness

the remaining   s
.

old man   a cigarette
told me his troubles
and
he said:

Pity

JACK HABEGGER

Cat Walk Shakes

private
flame
poor
conceited comedians.

Known
by gray man
who fondles
the night
longer
than all
bomb throats
in a

smoke cloud
cat walk shakes
like wax: pines
and our consciousness
the remaining

old man a cigarette
told me his troubles
and
he said:
Pity

SOURCE: "Poem for Personnel Managers" (poem), page 265, *The Pleasures of the Damned* (Ecco, 2007).

Impossible!

Arty

backstreets of Nowhere.

I ▮ hear ▮ narling ▮ ▮ *aren't you?*

tired and wet ▮

weariness ▮

keep me going—

long ▮

endless ▮ I ▮ flipped ▮ ure enough,

h the last match ▮

k toward ▮ the west ▮ the west ▮ the ▮ system couldn't handle ▮ it ▮

28

MARK HABEGGER

Impossible

Dirty backstreets of Nowhere,
I hear snarling,
tired and wet . . .
weariness.

Keep me going—
long, endless.
I flipped,
sure enough
the last match toward
the west.

The system couldn't handle it.

SOURCE: *Post Office* (novel), page 28, (Black Sparrow Press, 2002).

hands,

limbs in
the mouth   eyes

        a farce,

god,   puke out my
heart

Christ, stop
the
        darkness

there's no answer

ARA HARRIS

Screaming Prayer

Hands
Limbs in the mouth
Eyes
A farce
God
Puke out my heart
Christ
Stop the darkness
There's no answer

SOURCE: "The Parade" (poem), page 158, *Bone Palace Ballet* (Ecco, 2002).

What A Writer

████████████████ cummings

████████ cut away ████

███ holiness ████

███ with charm

and ████

████████ sliced through the

███

████████████████

████████ withering

███████

tired

████

████████████████████

copyists.

████████████████

as ████████████

████████████████

███

████████ only

one

████████

████

one sun.

████████

MITCH HICKS

What a Writer

cummings
cut away
holiness
with charm
and
sliced through the

withering
tired

copyists
as

only
one

one sun.

SOURCE: "What a writer" (poem), found at poemhunter.com.

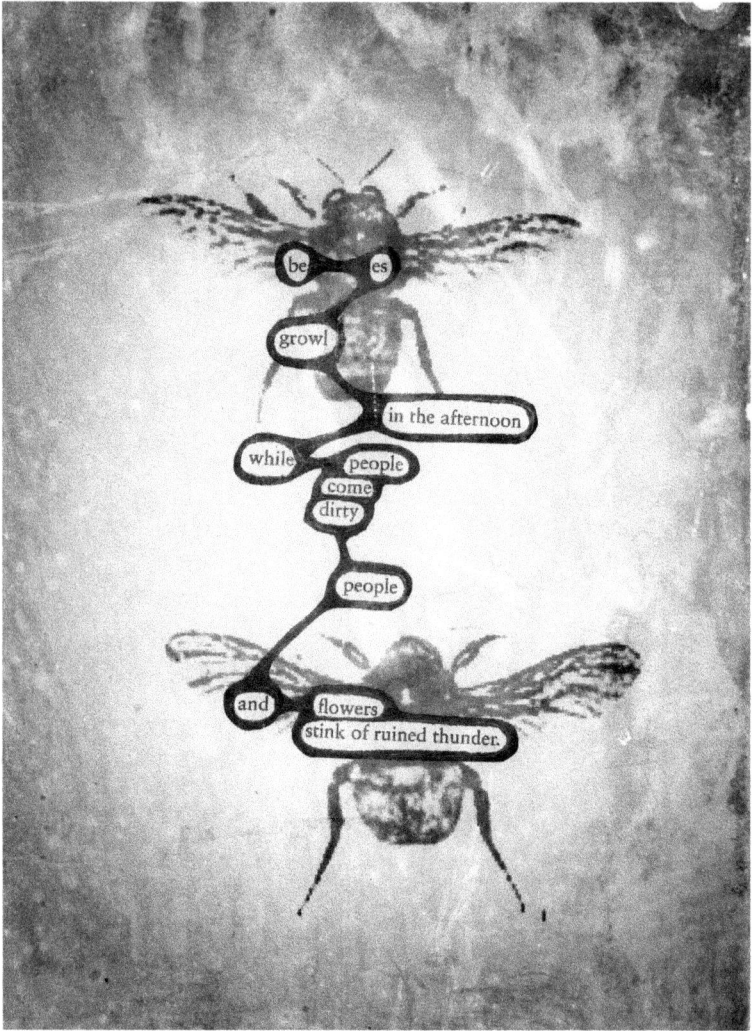

be es

growl

in the afternoon

while people
come
dirty

people

and flowers
stink of ruined thunder.

WM. TODD KING

Drones

Bees growl
in the afternoon
while people come.
Dirty people and flowers
stink of ruined thunder.

SOURCE: "Beast." (poem), page 234, *What Matters Most Is How Well You Walk through the Fire*. (Black Sparrow, 1999).

what

mad
lives   mutilate

ideal

homes
doors   open   close

behind the dying

still alive

wind
agony

ignorance.

a dog   a fence.

a man   at the window.

LAURIE KOLP

Addiction

What mad lives
mutilate ideal homes?
Doors open, close;
(behind) the dying
still alive, wind
agony, ignorance—
a dog, a fence, a man
at the window.

SOURCE: "hello, how are you" (poem), page 313, *The Night Torn Mad with Footsteps* (Black Sparrow Press, 2001).

cockroach

██████████ crouched
against the tile
████████████████████
██████████████
██████████
████████
I ██████████████
███████████████
██████████████████
██████ fell down ████
████████████
████ dying
████████████████
████ he didn't.
████████████████
███████████████████
██████ that's all there
was to that, ████
████████████████
██████████████
██████████
███████████████
████████████
██████████████
████████████
██████████

Paula J. Lambert

The Roach's Response

Crouched against the tile,
I fell down dying.
He didn't.
That's
all there was
to that.

SOURCE: "Cockroach" (poem), page 105, *Love Is a Dog from Hell* (Ecco, 2002).

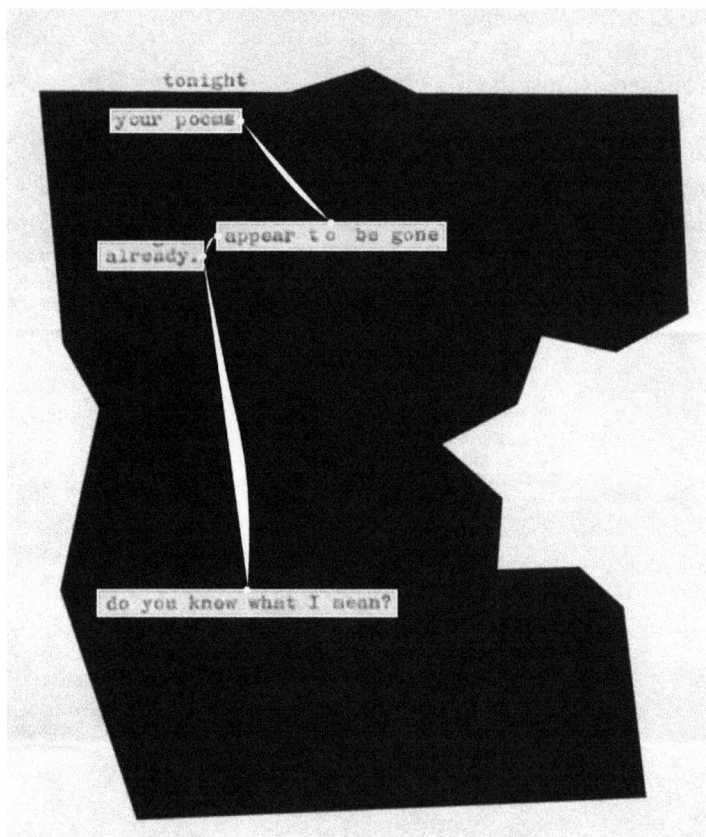

tonight
your poems
appear to be gone
already.
do you know what I mean?

ALEXANDER LIMAREV

tête-à-tête

tonight
your poems
appear to be gone
already.
do you know what I mean?

SOURCE: "tonight" (poem), 1972 manuscript.

fu se

I rive the night

and sit and look at the burned-down amusement pier
wonder why just sit

I want out

erased

that pier should er s

the burned-out guts

of my eyes,
a tomb in the sea.

madmen can
crawl into.

KAREN MASSEY

fuse

I rive the night
and sit and look
at the burned-down amusement pier
wonder why
just sit
I want out
erased

that pier shoulders
the burned-out guts
of my eyes
a tomb in the sea
madmen can
crawl into

SOURCE: "funhouse" (poem) page 258, *The Pleasures of the Damned: Poems, 1951-1993* (HarperCollins, 2007).

the ▬ grace, the end ▬
▬ eye in the ▬ bottle
is yours
▬
▬ voices, ▬ songs become a
snake ▬ crawls
away.

men go mad ▬.
▬
what else is there ▬
I ▬ have done it.

▬ the bottle
▬
it's ▬ a trick▬
everything is▬
▬ something ▬.
▬ where▬
▬
▬ here▬
▬ there▬

slowly one drinks ▬
▬ like a
lover▬

I weary of ▬ myself▬
▬ the only sport in
town.

CATFISH MCDARIS

fillet of buk

the grace, the end,
eye in the bottle
is yours

voices, songs
become a snake
crawls away

men go mad
what else is there
I have done it

the bottle, it's a
trick, everything
is something

where
here
there

slowly one
drinks
like a lover

I weary of
myself, the only
sport in town.

SOURCE: "the escapade of illusion" (poem), page 25, *Stovepiper, Book One* (Stovepiper Books. 1994).

at night

play the violin

with a hatchet

in the rain

GEORGE McKIM

friendly advice

at night
play the violin
with a hatchet
in the rain

SOURCE: "Friendly advice to a lot of young men," page 184, *The Rooming-house Madrigals: Early Selected Poems 1946-1966* (Black Sparrow Press, 1988).

I should go nude

Try to forget everything I should go box-
ing beat the shit out of
trouble and pain alive

under this elephant
one of the biggest ever

I awaken

out of it
paying excessively

frightened
of crap like that fright-
ened about
nothing more things are just what
they seem that's all there is to
the dreamer in your
pocket a good
hit cold ears a
little better feel my brain warm up
rapid decay
all the same
take hell out of here.
The man never carried
extra luggage The rest of us dump our
junk just to

see in reverse
Nirvana leaps into your lap

DE NAVARRO

In Reverse

I should go nude—try to forget everything
I should go boxing—beat the shit out of
trouble and pain.

Alive under this elephant (one of the biggest ever)
I awaken out of it paying excessively
frightened of crap like that
frightened about nothing more.

Things are just what they seem:
that's all there is to the dreamer in your pocket.

A good hit
      cold ears
a little better
      feel my brain
warm up
      rapid decay
all the same
      take hell
out of here.

The man never carried extra luggage,
the rest of us dump our junk just to see.

In reverse, Nirvana leaps into *your* lap.

SOURCE: *Pulp* (novel), page 103 (Ecco 2002).

this is

critical

critical

dangerous   dangerous

too many

too much

I intend

I intend

to

escape

KELLY NELSON

this is

critical

critical

dangerous

dangerous

too many

too much

I intend

I intend

to

escape

SOURCE: "this is where they come for what's left of your soul" (poem), page 235, Come *On In!: New Poems* (HarperCollins, 2006).

               goldfish   circled   around
                                     heavy drapes

and

       my father,

         poor fish,

                               threw   the cat
and   smiled

RICHARD O'BRIEN

When I Was a Kid

goldfish
circled around heavy

drapes and my father,

poor fish,

threw the cat and smiled.

SOURCE: "A Smile to Remember" (poem), page 17, *The Pleasures of the Damned: Poems, 1951-1993* (Ecco, 2008).

She

Time passed. looked

I

closed the door.

held the
kiss!

between us.

and

said finally, "when are you going to leave?"

WINSTON PLOWES

tHE kISs

She looked
Time passed.

I closed the door.

Held the kiss between us
and said finally,
"when are you going to leave?"

SOURCE: *Women* (novel), page 6 (Virgin Books, 2009).

some dogs
dream

black shoes,
you always cursed when you drank,

you finally

been dead
28 years

you were the only one
who understood
the futility of

bones
this dog
still
dreams about.

DAVID S. POINTER

Some dogs

dream

    black shoes

you finally

           been dead

28 years

you were the only one
who understood
the futility of

    bones

this dog

still

dreams about

SOURCE: "Eulogy to a Hell of a Dame" (poem), page 175, *The Pleasures of the Damned: Poems 1951-1993* (Ecco, 2008).

Alone

the bone
mind
in

a soul,
break
s   walls

one
keep

in and out
of

flesh.

:
a trapped
fate

finds
one.
the   dumps

nothing else

SHEIKHA A.

Alone

the bone
mind
in
a soul
breaks
walls
one
keep
in and out
of
flesh:
a trapped
fate
finds
one
the dumps
nothing else

SOURCE: "Alone with Everybody" (poem), page 97, *Love Is a Dog From Hell* (Ecco, 2002).

want

bursting out

unasked

you   sit for hours
staring
hunched over

searching for words,

trying to

forget about it,

consumed

your soul like

murder,

burning your gut,

until you die or it dies

SCOTT STOLLER

want

bursting out
unasked
you sit for hours
staring
hunched over
searching for words,
trying to
forget about it,
consumed,
your soul like
murder,
burning your gut,
until you die or it dies

SOURCE: "so you want to be a writer" (poem), page 3, *sifting through the madness for the Word, the line, the way* (Ecco, 2002).

I opened the door   and there she lay

my love

I was

like God
          when she was awake
she

of course,   was wise enough   to believe
this   and said,

this is the way love works, you see.   we   sat there

perfectly satisfied

                                she   left

          walked up the alley

and I turned in

KEYNA THOMAS

I opened the door

and there she lay

my love

I was like God

when she was awake

she of course,

was wise enough

to believe this and said,

this is the way love works, you see

we sat there

perfectly satisfied

she left

walked up the alley

and I turned in

SOURCE: "I Love You" (poem), page 51, *Play the Piano Drunk Like a Percussion Instrument Until the Fingers Begin to Bleed a Bit* (Ecco, 2003).

a

trick

I had this   sack   and

if you man-

aged

your time

this big

big

big   big   big

island far away and
lived in this little house

wrote   on a piece of paper.

talk

half the time

MELANIE VILLINES

a trick

I had this sack and
if you man-
aged
your time
this big
big
big big big
island faraway and
lived in this little house
wrote on a piece of paper
talk
half the time.

SOURCE: *Post Office* (novel), page 13 (Ecco, 2007).

Almost ██████ Poe█

blue hands, no ███ hands ████
████████ the fountain is ██ France
██ you wrote ██ that ████

████ insane ████████
████ artists ████
were your lovers, ████ it's all █
█ hea██ t█████ I'm not jealous
████ half █
████████, ███████,
████ worried about
██████ the █████ girl
████ who ████████ wake █ s
in the morning ████████
AN█ ███████ D ██████ is dead, █████
█ but listen ████ I was █
█ the ██████
best female poet ████ publishe█
█ d █ "████ she's mad ████
magic █ ███ no lie █ her fire █
████████ touches, ████
████████ graphs ████ have
████ more █ d sat █████ a
████ and listened ████
██████████
████████████ I
█ betray ████
█ a ██ bench █████ by a bridge ██
████ over a river ████ crying
████ night ██ wept for █ lovers ████
hurt and forgotten ██ I ████ never
heard again. ████████ suicide
████████████
█ would probably ██ be ████
██████ like this.

Ch████ uk██ ki

MERCEDES WEBB-PULLMAN

Almost Poe

Blue hand, no hands.
The fountain is France.
You wrote that insane artists
were your lovers;
it's all heat. I'm not jealous,
half worried about the girl
who wakes in the morning
and is dead. But listen
I was the best female poet,
published "She's mad
magic, no lie. Her fire touches."
Little graphs would have more
if I'd sat and listened.
That didn't happen. Sadder,
I betray a bench by a bridge
over a river, crying.
Night wept for lovers
hurt and forgotten. I never
heard again. Suicide
would probably
be like this.

SOURCE: "An Almost Made Up Poem" (poem), page 47, *Love is a Dog from Hell* (Black Sparrow Press, 1977).

maybe ███████████ all right

███████████████
█████ the oceans ██████████ have
consumed
████████████████████
████████████ as I continue to
consume—while
the ███████████ graveyards are
filled with ████████
███████ night ████████████
████████████████
████ roaring in ███ glee ███
████████ curling into a
tiny ████
█████████████████
eyed miracle.

the gods have been kind ███ through this
███████████
████████
█████████████████ gnawing
inside of me
███████
████████
███████
█████████

ZACHARY WEBER

Miracle

maybe I'm all right.
the oceans have consumed
as I continue to consume—
while the graveyards are filled
with night, roaring
in glee, curling
into a tiny-eyed
miracle.

the gods have been kind
through this gnawing
inside of me.

SOURCE: "I'll Take It" (poem), page 107, *You Get So Alone at Times that It Just Makes Sense* (HarperCollins 2002).

through ▚▚▚▚▚▚▚▚

of course it is nonsense to ▚▚▚▚▚
▚▚▚▚▚▚▚▚▚▚▚▚▚
▚▚▚▚▚▚▚▚▚▚▚▚
▚▚▚▚▚▚▚▚▚▚▚▚
▚▚▚▚▚▚▚▚

▚▚▚▚▚▚ read the newspapers,
▚▚▚▚▚▚▚▚▚
▚▚▚▚▚

like a ▚▚▚ poet on his last ▚▚▚
▚▚
▚▚▚▚▚▚
▚▚▚▚▚▚▚▚▚▚
▚▚▚▚▚▚▚

warm beer, ▚▚▚▚▚▚
disbelieving ▚▚▚▚▚▚
▚▚▚▚▚▚▚▚▚▚▚
▚▚▚▚▚▚▚▚

▚▚▚▚▚ death
▚▚▚▚▚▚▚▚▚
▚▚▚▚▚,
and the radio ▚▚▚▚
▚▚▚▚▚▚▚▚▚▚▚
▚▚▚▚▚▚▚▚▚▚
▚▚▚▚▚▚▚▚▚▚
▚▚▚▚▚▚▚▚▚▚
▚▚▚▚▚▚▚▚▚▚▚
▚▚▚▚▚▚▚▚▚.

THERESA WILLIAMS

through

of course it is nonsense to
read the newspapers
like a poet on his last
warm beer,
disbelieving
death
and the radio

SOURCE: "through the streets of anywhere" (poem), page 36, *Play the Piano Drunk Like a Percussion Instrument Until the Fingers Begin to Bleed a Bit* (Black Sparrow Press, 1994).

tragedy

I awakened   dead,

                    like bled corpses
surrounded   with their
    sun
                          cracked   and
undemanding
                                  a jester
with jokes upon absurd
                    nothing

        who had once been young

    the tragedy of
            the dead

                    stood
execrating and final,

    screaming
screaming
                    failed

BIRGIT ZARTL

tragedy

I awakened dead,
like bled corpses
surrounded with their
sun
cracked and
undemanding
a jester
with jokes upon absurd
nothing
who had once been young
the tragedy of
the dead
stood
execrating and final
screaming
screaming
failed

SOURCE: "The Tragedy of the Leaves" (poem), page 159, *The Pleasures of the Damned: Poems 1951-1993* (Ecco, 2008).

DAWNS

pure description

entails

savagery and

unschool s a prodigal worm

as overpowering
as   perfume on a sweating whore
                          artists

are quite vulgar and brashily sexy

when they

readjust

the microscopic vision

from   underground

magazines

ALI ZNAIDI

Bellowing Dawns

pure description

    entails

savagery and

      unschools a prodigal worm

                as overpowering
as   perfume on a sweating whore
               artists

are quite vulgar and brashily sexy

when they

      readjust

     the microscopic vision

from   underground

magazines

SOURCE: "So Much For The Knifers, So Much For The Bellowing Dawns" (poem), page 5, *Nomad* 5/6, Winter-Spring 1960.

NOTES FROM THE AUTHORS

SUZANNA ANDERSON: I fell in love with *Newspaper Blackout* by Austin Kleon. Creating my own blackout poems from newspapers and random text elated me. Now I'm working on a poetry project that cuts out words from my favorite band's lyrics and rearranges them into poems. With *Betting on the Muse: Poems & Stories* by Charles Bukowski in hand, I picked random stories and poems to create my poems. I used a purple or blue Crayola marker for my poems. Sometimes for my erasure poems I will use a Sharpie, but I don't like smelling them for long periods of time, so I use Crayola markers instead.

DAVID BARKER: I first read Charles Bukowski when I was in high school during the mid-1960s. My older brother brought home copies of underground newspapers he'd picked up in Los Angeles, and in these I was naturally drawn to Bukowski's scandalous and hilarious column, "Notes of A Dirty Old Man." I had no idea he was also an accomplished and widely published poet and short story writer until later when I was an undergraduate at CSULB in the late '60s. A fellow student, poet John Kay, tipped me off about Bukowski's masterful poetry. "He's the best thing out there," John claimed. It was true. John led me to professor Gerald Locklin, who taught English at the college. I sat in on Gerry's classes and was introduced to Bukowski's fiction. At his recommendation, I read *The Days Run Away Like Wild Horses Over the Hills* and *Post Office* when they first came out, and have been a huge fan of Bukowski ever since. Through Gerry, I met Bukowski and saw him read live on campus several times. If it hadn't been for John Kay and Gerald Locklin, I might never have known that Bukowski was far more than merely a cranky old columnist for a hippie rag. Or, at any rate, it would have taken me years to become aware of the extent of his literary genius. Locklin was an early and constant advocate for the importance of Bukowski's writing as a major cultural force at a time when Buk was largely dismissed by the rest of the academic world. Locklin deserves a lot of credit for seeing something in Bukowski that his peers in academia were blind to. History has proven him right. Bukowski is now an institution, a "classic" author. I found it tricky creating erasure poems from Buk's texts because just about every line is loaded with his unique voice, his down-to-earth message, and his distinctive outlook on life. It was a challenge to select words and phrases that would form a new narrative distinct from that of the source text.

ALESSANDRA BAVA: Bukowski's poetry has been a constant source of inspiration to me. He is one of those poets whose works I often read aloud ending up in laughter or tears. I selected "The Dangling Carrot," which plays with the idea that a perfect poem cannot be written. I am sure Bukowski truly meant it. As a poet, I find it hard to believe it possible—yet, sometimes I have been so close to writing a perfect poem that I decided to use Bukowski's to try to write one.

MELISSA ELEFTHERION: I read my first Bukowski book—*The Most Beautiful Girl in Town*—in my late teens. I found it at the old Tower Books and felt simultaneously attracted and repulsed by both this man and his text. Later, I learned from a clerk that Bukowski's books were stored behind the register in all other bookstores due to their high risk for being stolen. This fascinated me and served as a basis for further inquiry. While I have had a love/hate relationship with his writing, Bukowski's determination along with his distillation of the idea of a "writing cycle" (writing, revising, submitting, publishing) has fueled my efforts to keep churning stuff out year after year, and gain some sense of distance during the submission process. I've come to think of Bukowski as a cranky man on my side.

MARK ERICKSON: The building in the photo is along the waterfront near Jack London Square in West Oakland. A classic 1920s building and now an abandoned warehouse that once housed Adeline Cleaners. A gorgeous brick building that I shoot from time to time. Seemed fitting for the Bukowski poem I chose, "Something's Knocking at the Door." The name of the poem I adjusted to "A Great White Light" which fits well with what is happening around Oakland these past years, and the gorgeous light we are getting these days, as we head into fall.

S.A. GRIFFIN: Charles Bukowski has been a top favorite and major influence since first encountering his work in 1982. Over the years, he has inspired deeper feeling, much needed laughter, and has directed me to see my own work very differently. He is a light, a romantic, a survivor with his humanity intact. For me, the process of erasure is like taking a snapshot of the smile on the Mona Lisa, or picking an apple from the tree without harming the tree itself.

96

JACK HABEGGER: My Dad introduced me to Charles Bukowski's work at a young age. I really admire his style and word choice. I hope that my erasure poem reflects my appreciation of his craft.

MARK HABEGGER: Los Angeles has always had a strong influence on me. When I first moved west from rural Ohio, I think I quickly encountered an L.A. that was closer to Bukowski's vision of the city than the idealized one I had created in my mind. Creating a poem from the dissected body of Bukowski's work was my small tribute to that Los Angeles.

ARA HARRIS: Bukowski is my favorite poet. His gritty candid style and beautiful misuse of language are brilliant. No one can twist a phrase like Charles. I chose this poem because I saw a prayer and pain in it. I see prayer in a lot of Bukowski's work. I think he wanted to be saved from a world that didn't fit him.

PAULA J. LAMBERT: I had not known much about Bukowski's work until I met my husband, Michael, who had been a fan and owned several of his books. We started reading some of the poems aloud together, reading about Bukowski's difficult life history, look-ing for documentary films, and so on. Although I do like a lot of his work very much, I'm actually far more fascinated by Bukowski's bi-ography: the pain he was in and the pain he caused, all while creating a wealth of art. When I saw the *Bukowski on Wry* [bukowskion-wry.wordpress.com] call for erasure poems, I immediately pulled from the shelf a copy of *Love Is a Dog from Hell,* which I'd bought for Michael as a "wry" Valentine's Day/birthday gift the previous year. Nothing really clicked for me at first; I wasn't sure how the ex-ercise might play out until I turned to "cockroach" on page 105 and the insect who, after being "sprayed / and sprayed and sprayed" comes out of hiding to give the speaker "a very dirty look" before fal-ling onto his back and dying. That pissed-off roach is too vivid a character, too much like Bukowski himself, not to be given his say. "The Cockroach's Response" pretty much leapt from the lines.

DE NAVARRO: Charles Bukowski was a gruff man who champi-oned the gritty life of the inner city. Having come from the inner city myself I understand the rawness of daily life on the streets. What ap-peals to me most about his life and legacy is that he didn't care what others thought of him. He was going to make it happen no matter the opposition or struggle. His tenacity to barge his way into the literary world regardless of the resistance of academia is a dramatic story in itself, one that many can relate to. As soon as I learned about the erasure poem anthology, I decided I wanted to do something from the last book he published in his life—the novel, *Pulp*. I reread the novel and kept looking for that page that said something to me—that stood out as a page that had something to say to the world. On page 103 of the book I hit gold. It spoke of a boxing match, and immediately I thought about the boxing match of life—what if you were down and wanted to go beat up life? So I worked the page until I found the best way I knew to capture what I wanted. The process I used was simply to pull phrases and put phrases together and keep thinking of the whole, what I wanted it to say about this subject using these words on the page. It was a distinct challenge that I enjoyed and a fitting tribute to Bukowski in his style and character. The speaker in my poem is angry at life and considers going nude and forgetting everything, in other words, going back "in reverse" to the day he was born. He decides to go beat the shit out of his trouble and pain in a boxing match at the gym. So huge is this trouble and pain that he likens it to being under the weight of an elephant. At first he is cold, and pays dearly in the bout, but gets to the place that he is frightened by nothing more, so much for the dreamer. Having come to himself (psychologically nude), with nothing to lose, he comes back to life and bests his opponent. He attributes his win in a roundabout way to the strength he's gained by bearing his trouble and pain because he notes his opponent never carried the extra luggage that he's carried. By the end of the poem, he's dumped his junk and is now on top of the world, having licked his sparring partner and his trouble and pain—Nirvana has leapt into his lap.

RICHARD O'BRIEN: My first encounter with Charles Bukowski happened when I was twenty-two years old. A friend recommended *Dangling in the Tournefortia*. For me, a poet still feeling his way around—sometimes in the dark—Bukowski showed me the importance of making every word count. After that, I read everything by him. I chose for my erasure poem "When I was a Kid" Bukowski's poem "A Smile to Remember." It called to mind how people are always telling me I should smile more often as if such a thing was a cure-all—especially, in the face of the brutality we often witness in our lives. For the erasure process, I wanted to peel away enough to where I could turn the poem on its head, make it as surreal as possible—but then I thought that if it was too surreal perhaps Bukowski would have hated it or, better yet, liked it.

KEYNA THOMAS: I had heard of Charles Bukowski after I began writing for a living in 2006; sadly, several years passed before I really read his work. In 2010, I found myself sick, mostly bedridden, and exhausted. One night around 2011, still ill and not improving, I stumbled upon and watched a wonderful documentary, *Bukowski: Born Into This*. It opens with a shot of Bukowski preparing for a public reading. "Dennis, hey, Dennis," he says, "you're running this motherfucking show…" It wasn't more than ten minutes before I was hooked. In my sickened state, I had begun to feel numb and disconnected. Hearing him separated me from my physical pain and threw me violently back into awareness of my emotions and thoughts. At present, I am well, working, and writing. To me, Bukowski embodies everything ugly and everything beautiful about humanity. His work reflects these things in such a way that I feel uncomfortable and comforted at the same time. As I searched for words, it seemed natural to find the beauty in an ugly situation and make a humble attempt to offer comfort where there seemed to be so little.

MELANIE VILLINES: *Post Office* was my initiation into Bukowski. It is still my favorite of his many works. Maybe it's because three of my uncles worked for the U.S. Postal Service, and I know something about a postman's trials and tribulations.

THERESA WILLIAMS: I discovered Charles Bukowski in 1990 or so. I just know it was soon after I had finished my MFA. I found him at the now-defunct bookstore in Toledo, Ohio, called Thackerays. At that time, I was buying one poetry collection a month as a way of reviving my creative life, which had become quite dead. Bukowski's poems felt honest to me, and it had been a long time since I'd written anything that was honest. Maybe I never had. At any rate, his poems helped to salvage this drowned soul. I'm forever grateful.

ZACHARY WEBER: I've enjoyed creating erasures for quite some time, and was excited to take on the challenge of erasing Bukowski's poetry (which I've held in high esteem). I chose poems like "I'll Take It . . ." or "Fractional Note" because they are so dense with strong images. By stripping much of Bukowski's prose away, I was able to work with these bare images and create poems that were strikingly compact and unique.

ALI ZNAIDI: I chose Charles Bukowski's poem "So Much For The Knifers, So Much For The Bellowing Dawns" because I love his simple yet condensed and distilled language. The words of the poem are jubilantly dancing in the dance floor of the poem. The erasure poem was an exercise in joy, as I would continually cross out words that I found them not sweating too much in their dance. The poem took shape, and came to life with only those words I saw more energetic.

ABOUT THE AUTHORS

SUZANNA ANDERSON studied creative writing at Bowling Green State University. She participates in National Novel Writing Month every year. Her interests also include watercolor, charcoal, and book-binding. Currently, she is the editor-in-chief of *The Magnolia Review*.

TARA R. ANDREWS is an author of children's books. Her latest is *Ava & Bob*, available at Amazon.com.

BETH AYER is Senior Poetry Editor/Web Manager for the *Found Poetry Review*. Her work has appeared in publications including *Upstart*'s *Out of Sequence: The Sonnets Remixed, Otis Nebula, Imitation & Allusion, Of Zoos* (forthcoming), and the Silver Birch Press *NOIR Erasure Poetry Anthology*. Find her at bethayer.com and on Twitter @bethdayer.

JENNI B. BAKER is the found and editor-in-chief of The Found Poetry Review (foundpoetryreview.com). How own poetry (found and not) has been published in more than twenty literary journals. Visit her at jennibbaker.com.

DAVID BARKER'S short stories and poems have been published in dozens of small press chapbooks, little magazines, and anthologies in the U. S. and Europe since the early 1970s. In 2011, Bottle Of Smoke Press published his novel, *Death At The Flea Circus*, and another novel, *Stella Vero*, has been accepted by the same publisher. *Opal's Trails*, a book of short poems about nature diarist, Opal Whiteley, was published in the UK by Pig Ear Press during 2013. He is best known among Bukowski fans for his short 1982 memoir, *Charles Bukowski Spit In My Face*, which has been reissued as a Kindle ebook.

MARY BAST writes poetry, found poetry, and memoir. She was one of eighty-five poets from seven countries participating in 2013 National Poetry Month's Pulitzer Remix, and has recently published in *Bacopa Literary Review, Blue Monday Review, Connotation Press, Haunted Waters Press, Pea River Journal, right hand pointing, Six Minute Magazine, Survivor's Review*, and *The Found Poetry Review*. When Mary's hands are not on computer keys, they're holding brush to canvas, inspired by North Central Florida's woodlands, lakes, and prairies.

ALESSANDRA BAVA lives and works in the Eternal City [Rome, Italy]. She holds an MA in American Literature, and she manages her own translation agency. Her poems have appeared in journals such as *Plath Profiles, Thrush Poetry Journal, Empty Mirror,* and *Left Curve.* She is the author of two bilingual chapbooks *Nocturne* (Edizioni Pulcinoelefante, 2013) and *Guerilla Blues* (Edizioni Ensemble, 2012), both published in Italy. Her first U.S.-published chapbook, *They Talk About Death,* is available from Blood Pudding Press. Her forthcoming chapbook, *Diagnosis,* will be released by Dancing Girl Press in 2014. She is the editor of *Rome's Revolutionary Poets Brigade Anthology Vol 1* (Edizioni Ensemble, 2012) and *Articolo 1* (Edizioni Albeggi, 2014). She is currently writing the biography of a contemporary American poet.

BRINDA BULJORE is a writer living in Paris, France.

KATHY BURKETT is a high school dropout who eventually earned a B.A. in English/creative writing. She lives in Florida with her beloved husband and pets. Her writing has been previously published by *The Red Fez, Menacing Hedge, Thirteen Myna Birds, Bacopa, Gutter Eloquence, Nerve Cowboy, Right Hand Pointing,* and other small press publications. In addition to writing, she enjoys playing kazoo for adoring audiences of stuffed animals, cloud watching, and singing with her hound dog.

TOBI COGSWELL is a four-time Pushcart nominee and a Best of the Net nominee. Credits include or are forthcoming in various journals in the U.S., U.K., Sweden, and Australia. In 2012 and 2013, she was short-listed for the Fermoy International Poetry Festival. In 2013, she received Honorable Mention for the Rachel Sherwood Poetry Prize. Her sixth and latest chapbook is *Lapses & Absences* (Blue Horse Press). Her seventh chapbook *The Coincidence of Castles* is forthcoming from Glass Lyre Press. She is the coeditor of San Pedro River Review (sprreview.com).

SUBHANKAR DAS is a poet, film producer, bookstore owner, and publisher of Bangla experimental material. He produced six short films that have been honored at international film festivals, and has trans- lated the works Allen Ginsberg and Charles Bukowski into Bangla. *Thieves of the Wind,* his poetry chapbook jointly written with Catfish McDaris, is now available from Writing Knights Press.

MELISSA ELEFTHERION grew up in Brooklyn. She is the author of *huminsect* (dancing girl press), *prism maps* (dusie kollektiv), *Pigtail Duty* (forthcoming from dancing girl press), and several other chapbooks and fragments. She holds an MLIS from San Jose State

University, and an MFA from Mills College. Recent work appears or is forthcoming in *Bibliomancy Oracle, Bone Bouquet, {carriage return}, Dusie, Finery, Open Letters Monthly, Poet as Radio,* and *So to Speak.* She lives and works as a teen librarian in Ukiah, California, where she creates poetry programming and also manages the Poetry Center Chapbook Exchange.

MARK ERICKSON was born in Hollywood, California, and lives along the West Coast of United States. After growing up in Hollywood, his family moved to Germany and Italy. He later settled in the Bay Area to study painting and art history at the San Francisco Art Institute and the San Francisco Art Academy. Mark paints in his studio in California and exhibits in galleries around the United States. He continues writing poetry and short stories that often are inspiration for his paintings. He has self-published numerous books on painting, photography, and poetry in collaboration with Katy Zartl of Katworks Graphics in Vienna, Austria. He is presently working on a photo book, *The Man From Painted Woods,* of his father's exploits in World War II. You can view Mark's work at markerickson.com.

ALEXIS RHONE FANCHER's work can (or soon will) be found in *Rattle, The MacGuffin, Carnival Lit Magazine, Fjords Review, Cliterature, The Chiron Review, Good Men Project, Deep Water Literary Journal, Poeticdiversity, Little Raven, This Is Poetry: Women of the Small Presses, Gutter Eloquence, Slipstream, The Mas Tequila Review, Broadzine!, H_NGM_N,* and *Wide Awake,* The Pacific Coast Poetry Series forthcoming anthology of Los Angeles poets. Her photographs have been published worldwide. She is the author of *How I Lost My Virginity To Michael Cohen and Other Heart Stab Poems* (Sybaritic Press, 2014). Since 2013, Alexis has been nominated for two Pushcart Prizes and a Best of The Net award. She is poetry editor of *Cultural Weekly.* Find her online at alexisrhonefancher.com.

S.A. GRIFFIN is a universe in sleep's clothing.

JACK HABEGGER is the artist and writer behind the ongoing comic strip *Peachy Clinker.* Visit him online at facebook.com/jackhabeggerartist.

MARK HABEGGER is the father of cartoonist Jack Habegger. He has worked in various capacities in the entertainment industry, and is best known as the special effects manager for the Jim Jarmusch film *Dead Man.* He lives with his wife and son in Southern California.

ARA HARRIS is a poet and the indie music/art editor at virago-mag.com. She self-published a full collection of poetry in 2012 titled *Original Soundtrack Not Available*. One reader described the book as, "A Tom Verlaine riff in every synapse." Basically her work is like pulling the veil off of suburbia to unearth reality. She wrote poetry before she read any. She thinks that was the best choice that she could have made. Music, love, sex, emotion, and the human condition are her inspiration.

MITCH HICKS: There are only two dates in his bios, born 1957 London and death yet uncut. The stuff in-between may well rise up, but for now it's maybe modest in life and outrages in death. It's for others to dig deep and unearth, he's just happy to observe life in the way he does!

WM. TODD KING is a found-text poet bringing old words to new tongues in the rolling green of Kentucky. He is the recent finalist in the Found Poetry Review's Dog Ear Poetry Contest, and a participant in 2013's Pulitzer Remix project. His works have appeared recently in *Short Fast & Deadly,* Silver Birch Press *NOIR Erasure Poetry Anthology, Socio Poetic, Lá Bloom*, and *Potroast*.

LAURIE KOLP is an award-winning poet with more than three dozen publications worldwide. Her first full-length poetry collection, *Upon the Blue Couch*, was published by Winter Goose Publishing in 2014 and is available on Amazon. Learn more about Laurie on her website at lauriekolp.com.

PAULA J. LAMBERT is a member of the Ohio Arts Council Arts Learning Program and the author of two books of poetry—*The Sudden Seduction of Gravity* (Full/Crescent Press, 2012) and *The Guilt That Gathers* (Pudding House, 2009). She is a past recipient of an Ohio Arts Council Individual Artist Fellowship and was a resident fellow at the Virginia Center for Creative Arts. Lambert's MFA in Creative Writing is from Bowling Green State University. She currently resides in Dublin, Ohio, with her husband Michael Perkins, with whom she operates Full/Crescent Press, a small but growing independent publisher of poetry books and broadsides.

ALEXANDER LIMAREV is a freelance artist, mail art artist, and poet who lives in Russia—with artwork found in private and museum collections in forty countries. His artwork and poetry have appeared in a variety of online publications, including *Time for A Vispo, Expoesia Visual Experimental #9, #10, The New Post-Literate: A Gallery of*

Asemic Writing, BAA: BE: L, Nothing and Insight, Foffof, Spontaneous Combusions Language Image Lab, Fooom, Poezine, Degu: A Journal of Signs #1, Existere, The White Raven #11, Undergroundbooks.org, OOooo #1, and Boek861, Tip of the Knife #15, Kiosko #7, and *Microlit #7.*

KAREN MASSEY is a writer and artisan who lives in Ottawa, Canada. Her work has won varied prizes and has appeared in numerous literary journals and anthologies including *Decalogue: Ten Ottawa Poets* (Chaudiere Books). She has written one chapbook, *bullet* (above/ground press), and her recent erasure poetry has been published online at Bukowski on Wry, Bywords.ca, and Ottawater.ca, as well as in the Silver Birch Press *May Poetry Anthology*. Her erasure poetry recently appeared in *Lá Bloom,* a special online issue of *The Found Poetry Review* featuring poetry sourced from James Joyce's *Ulysses.*

CATFISH MCDARIS's most infamous chapbook is *Prying* with Jack Micheline and Charles Bukowski. He's done over twenty chaps in the last twenty-five years. He is an aging New Mexican living near Milwaukee. He has four walls, a ceiling, heat, food, a woman, a daughter, two cats, a typing machine, and a mailbox.

GEORGE MCKIM has an MFA in Painting. He began writing poetry at the age of fifty-six and his work has appeared or is forthcoming in *Diagram, elimae, The Found Poetry Review, Dear Sirs, Shampoo, Ditch, Cricket Online Review, Otoliths, Blaze Vox, Poets and Artists Magazine*, The Tupelo Press 30/30 Project, and others. His chapbook of found poetry, *Found & Lost*, will be published by Silver Birch Press in November 1014.

DE NAVARRO was born in Newport, Rhode Island, but grew up in inner city Chicago, then rural Crown Point, Indiana, and finally suburban Munster, Indiana, until he went to college. His love of poetry and the writing arts began at age eight, and in 1980 he was a featured poet in the *Purdue Exponent*. Many of his poems have since been published in various magazines, publications, literary journals, anthologies, and online. In 2009, he compiled and produced the poetry anthology *Between Life and Language*. His second and current book, *Dare to Soar* (2013) features a diverse collection of his poems. He lives in the Greater Los Angeles area (Bukowski-land), where he continues to be an avid writer, poet, and editor.

KELLY NELSON is the author of *Rivers I Don't Live By*, winner of the 2013 Concrete Wolf Chapbook Award. Her found poetry has appeared in *Really System, Verbatim, Found Poetry Review,* and an NPR/PBS anthology *The Liberal Media Made Me Do It.* She received a grant from the Arizona Commission on the Arts in support of a book-length found poetry project based on her uncle's five-hundred-page prison record. A Pushcart Prize and Best of the Net nominee, she holds a PhD in Anthropology and teaches Inter-disciplinary Studies at Arizona State University.

RICHARD J. O'BRIEN's poems have appeared in *Stoneboat, New Plains Review, Falling Star Magazine,* and other publications. A gradu-ate of Fairleigh Dickinson University MFA in Creative Writing Program, Richard teaches English composition and literature at Mercer County Community College, Rowan University, and Temple University.

WINSTON PLOWES is a teacher, compere, performer, and poet, who spends his days fine-tuning background noise and rescuing dis-carded words. These are re-sculpted over a glass of wine into poetry birds he releases by night to fly to new homes in poetry journals and online destinations worldwide. He lives in a floating home in Hebden Bridge, West Yorkshire, UK, where he tries to persuade his two black cats that it's a good idea for them to do the same.

DAVID S. POINTER currently serves on the advisory panel at "Writing For Peace." His work has appeared or is forthcoming in Sil-ver Birch Press anthologies including *Bukowski* (2013), *NOIR Era-sure* (2013), and *The Great Gatsby* (2015). David's latest collection of poetry is entitled *Oncoming Crime Facts*, available at lulu.com.

SHEIKHA A. currently lives in Karachi, Pakistan after having moved from the United Arab Emirates and believes the transition has definitely stimulated a different tunnel of thought. With publi-cation credits in magazines such as *Red Fez, American Diversity Report, Open Road Review, Mad Swirl, Danse Macabre du Jour, Rose Red Review, The Penmen Review* among many others, and several anthologies, she has also authored a poetry collection enti-tled *Spaced*, published by Hammer and Anvil Books, available on Kindle. She also edits poetry for eFiction India. Visit her blog at sheikha82.wordpress.com.

SCOTT STOLLER's work has appeared in many online and print journals and anthologies including *Weave, decomP, Prick of the Spin-dle*, and *Best Contemporary Tanka*. He's a physician in the west suburbs of Chicago.

KEYNA THOMAS is a freelance writer of poetry and short stories, as well as a part-time administrative assistant at a state university, where she is working on her Bachelor's. She has worked in New England as a reporter and staff writer for MediaNews Group. There, she learned that true stories about people are almost always as interesting as fiction. Since then she has been writing a short novel that merges the two. Keyna grew up in Central Massachusetts, where she now lives and works. She and some of her 140-character (or less) ramblings can be found at twitter.com/Keyna.

MELANIE VILLINES is a writer who lives in Los Angeles.

MERCEDES WEBB-PULLMAN received a MA in Creative Writing from Victoria University Wellington New Zealand. Her work has appeared in a range of journals, including *Turbine, 4th Floor, Swamp, Reconfigurations, The Electronic Bridge, poetryrepairs, Connotations, The Red Room,* and in books such as *Numeralla Dreaming, After the Danse, Food 4 Thought, Looking for Kerouac, Ono,* and *Bravo Charlie Foxtrot.*

ZACHARY WEBER is studying creative writing at the University of Houston. An assistant poetry editor in the school's undergraduate journal, *Glass Mountain,* his work has appeared in its college journal *The Aletheia.*

THERESA WILLIAMS keeps a blog called "The Letter Project." Her novel, *The Secret of Hurricanes,* was a finalist for the Paterson Fiction Prize, and her stories and poems have appeared in *Apple Valley Review, Gargoyle, Hunger Mountain, The Sun,* and many other magazines.

BIRGIT ZARTL is a painter and photographer based in Vienna, Austria. Her main interest lies in subconscious symbolism and imagery. Visit her at birgitzartl.com.

ALI ZNAIDI (b. 1977) lives in Redeyef, Tunisia, where he teaches English. He graduated with a BA in Anglo-American Studies in 2002 from the University of Sfax (Tunisia). He writes poetry and has an interest in literature, languages, and literary translation. His work has appeared in various magazines and journals worldwide. He has authored four poetry chapbooks, including *Experimental Ruminations* (Fowlpox Press, 2012); *Moon's Cloth Embroidered with Poems* (Origami Poems Project, 2012); *Bye, Donna Summer!* (Fowlpox Press, 2014); and *Taste of the Edge* (Kind of A Hurricane Press, 2014). Links to his published and forthcoming works can be found at aliznaidi.blogspot.com.

ABOUT THE COVER ARTIST

Loren Kantor is a passionate, curious woodcutter/writer living in Hollywood with a love for movies, music, and old Los Angeles. Find out more about Loren and his work at woodcuttingfool.blogspot.com.

www.ingramcontent.com/pod-product-compliance
Lightning Source LLC
Chambersburg PA
CBHW070641030426
42337CB00020B/4110